Cover design by: Kronos Mond

GRASSHOPPER AND MR OX

By Elizabeth Russell

"Hello Mr Ox, how are you today?
Would you like to come and play?"

"Hello Grasshopper,
are you sure!?
We can't play,
you're too close to the floor"

"Ah Mr Ox, but haven't you heard,
I can fly high,
as high as a bird!"

"Oh' Grasshopper I'm too strong,
I can pull twelve hundred pounds!
Now please run along."

"Mr Ox I'm strong too,
my legs are long,
and can jump over you!"

"Grasshopper can't you see,
I'm way too big,
as big as this tree!"

"Well Mr Ox,
being small is great,
I have much more to explore,
you should be my mate."

"Grasshopper;
I'm brown and hairy,
you'll get lost,
you should be wary."

"Mr Ox don't you worry,
I'm as green as the grass,
you'll find me in a hurry."

"Hmm Grasshopper,
I won't hear you speak,
when we run,
we have very loud feet!"

"Mr Ox,
you should hear us cheer,
we chime all night,
always so clear."

"Ha! Grasshopper,
I'm too fast,
our hoofs rumble,
you will surely be last."

"Mr Ox!
I'm not here to race,
just a lovely game,
at an equal pace."

"Oh goodness me,
I'm big, you're small,
now just leave me be!"
Mr Ox paused, Grasshopper stood tall.

"Mr Ox you are mighty fine,
have a nice day,
I'll see you another time."

The next day Mr Ox woke up,
he looked left, he looked right,
and saw no one in sight.

No one to play, or say *'have a nice day'*.

Mr Ox felt sad, and knew he had been bad.

He marched and marched but Grasshopper
could not be found.
He looked up, he looked down but Grasshopper
was not around.

Mr Ox stopped, and stood.
Feeling so lost in the wood.

"Mr Ox!?
I'm trying to sleep!
Your hoofs are loud,
you should learn how to creep."

Mr Ox looked up, he looked down and looked all around.
But Grasshopper could not be found.

"Oh Mr Ox,
I told you I was strong,
I jumped up on your head,
I've been here all along!"

"Grasshopper,
I'm so sorry,
I do want to play,
can we have a nice day!?"

"Ah, Mr Ox,
I have the best game of all,
Hide and seek!
It's great to be big and it's great to be small."

Grasshopper and Mr Ox spent the rest
of the day hiding and seeking.

It became their most favourite game.

Grasshopper and Mr Ox remain friends to this day.

The End.

ABOUT THE AUTHOR

Elizabeth Russell

"Elizabeth Russell is a bestselling author of Grasshopper and Mr Ox, the first book in a series called 'Unlikely Friends'. Miss Russell, her partner and many pets call the Surrey area in the UK home. You can visit her online at www.RussellBooks.co.uk or on Instagram @RussellBooks"

Printed in Great Britain
by Amazon

15392966R00020